The Science of Living Things

What is a
BEAR?

Bobbie Kalman & John Crossingham

Crabtree Publishing Company

www.crabtreebooks.com

The Science of Living Things Series
A Bobbie Kalman Book

(Dedicated by John Crossingham)
To Liam Tully - the newest lil' cub

Editor-in-Chief
Bobbie Kalman

Writing team
Bobbie Kalman
John Crossingham

Editor
Amanda Bishop

Copy editors
Niki Walker
Kate Calder
Heather Levigne

Computer design
Kymberley McKee Murphy

Production coordinator
Heather Fitzpatrick

Photo researcher
John Crossingham

Consultant
Richard B. Harris, Ph.D., Editor, *Ursus*
Research Associate, Wildlife Biology
Program, University of Montana

Photographs
Frank S. Balthis: pages 5 (top), 16 (top), 17 (bottom), 22,
    23 (both), 24
Robert McCaw: pages 10 (top), 11, 12, 14 (both), 20,
    21 (bottom), 28 (bottom), 29
Tom Stack & Associates: Erwin and Peggy Bauer: pages 4, 27;
    Jeff Foott: pages 15, 18 (bottom)
    Victoria Hurst: pages 1, 10 (bottom), 21 (top)
    Thomas Kitchin: pages 5 (bottom), 19 (top)
    Joe McDonald: page 31
Michael P. Turco: pages 9, 25 (both), 26, 30
Other images by Adobe Image Library and Digital Stock

Illustrations
Barbara Bedell: pages 6 (top left), 10, 14, 16 (right), 18,
    19, 21, 22, 23, 24, 25, 26, 29 (top left)
Antoinette DiBiasi: pages 12, 15 (top right)
Barb Hinterhoeller: page 13
Cori Marvin: page 11
Margaret Amy Reiach: pages 1 (flowers), 6 (top right,
    bottom left and right), 7, 9, 15 (top left), 16 (left), 17,
    28, 29 (middle and bottom)

Crabtree Publishing Company
www.crabtreebooks.com   1-800-387-7650

PMB16A
350 Fifth Avenue
Suite 3308
New York, NY
10118

612 Welland Avenue
St. Catharines
Ontario
Canada
L2M 5V6

73 Lime Walk
Headington
Oxford
OX3 7AD
United Kingdom

Cataloging in Publication Data
Kalman, Bobbie
    What is a bear?
        p. cm. -- (The Science of living things)
        Includes index.
        ISBN 0-86505-983-7 (RLB) ISBN 0-86505-960-8 (pbk.)
    This book introduces children to the physical characteristics
and behaviors of bears.
    1. Bears—Juvenile literature. [1. Bears.] I. Crossingham, John. II.
Title. III. Series: Kalman, Bobbie. Science of living things.
    QL737.C27 K353 2001
    599.78—dc21
                                                    LC00-069366
                                                    CIP

Contents

What is a bear?   4

The bear family   6

A bear's body   8

Bear behavior   10

Winter sleep   12

Caring for cubs   14

Polar bears   16

Brown bears   18

American black bears   20

Asiatic black bears   22

Sun bears   23

Spectacled bears   24

Sloth bears   25

Giant pandas   26

Bears and people   28

Bears in danger   30

Words to know & Index   32

What is a bear?

Bears belong to a group of animals called **mammals**. Their body is covered in fur and, like other mammals, bears are **warm-blooded**. The body temperature of warm-blooded animals stays the same in hot or cold places. A female bear carries her young inside her body until they are ready to be born. Her body makes milk to feed her babies.

Many places around the world are home to bears. Most bears live in forests and are great tree climbers. Larger bears, such as the Kodiak and grizzly, live on open, hilly plains near forests. The polar bear lives in the most remote region of all—the frozen ice caps of the Arctic. Bears can live as long as thirty years in the wild.

A bear has few natural enemies because it is so large and strong.

Living alone

Bears are **solitary** animals, which means they spend most of their life alone. Many people think that bears are fierce, but most are shy and peaceful. They would much rather leave an area than fight with a person or another bear. When two adult bears meet one another, the larger bear usually scares the other one away. The only time two grown bears stay close to each other is when a male and female are about to **mate** to make babies. A male bear is called a **boar**, and a female is called a **sow**.

Brainy bears

Bears are highly intelligent, curious animals. They can be trained to perform tasks and can learn from past experiences. Bears that live near humans often explore and feed in garbage dumps. They have learned that these areas provide a constant source of food. People have even seen bears placing a claw into a keyhole, trying to open a locked door to find food!

(above) These two male spectacled bears are fighting over a sow. The stronger bear will be the one to mate with her.

The bear family

There are eight different **species**, or kinds, of bears. Seven of these species belong to the animal family **Ursidae**. The one exception is the giant panda. Until recently, many scientists felt the panda was a relative of the raccoon. Today, most scientists feel that the giant panda is a bear.

Ancient ancestor

A small mammal called the **miacid** is believed to be the ancestor of bears. Miacids lived millions of years ago. They are also thought to be the ancestor of dogs and cats.

(above) There are a few types of brown bears. One type, the Kodiak, lives only on Kodiak Island in Alaska.

(above) American black bears live in forests across North America.

(right) The polar bear is the largest land-based **carnivore**, or animal that eats meat.

(left) The sloth bear's long curved claws are excellent for climbing, but they make walking on the ground an awkward experience.

The sun bear has a very long tongue, which it uses to eat honey and insects.

The Asiatic black bear lives in mountain forests.

The spectacled bear climbs trees to escape its enemies.

The giant panda sits on its haunches while it eats.

A bear's body

Like all mammals, bears belong to a large group of animals called **vertebrates**. Vertebrates are animals with a backbone. Fish, reptiles, birds, and amphibians are also vertebrates. Sun bears are the smallest bears, whereas polar bears and Kodiaks are the largest bears.

Bears have two layers of fur. A short layer of fur keeps the bear warm. A second layer of long **guard hairs** keeps water away from the short fur and skin of the bear.

Bears have a powerful roar, which they use to warn intruders to stay away from their territory.

Bears are **plantigrade** animals—their feet are flat on the ground when they walk. This position allows bears to stand and walk on their back legs.

The shape of a bear's claws depends on their use. Bears that dig, such as this grizzly, have straight claws. Climbing bears have curved claws that easily grip tree trunks.

Chew on this

A bear's teeth are well adapted to the animal's varied diet. At the front of its mouth, a bear has huge, sharp **canine** teeth. These teeth cut through animal flesh and allow a bear to tear off chunks of meat. At the back of its mouth are flat **molars**, which are used to grind plant material such as leaves, grasses, bark, and berries.

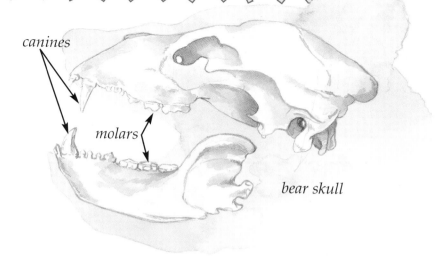

canines

molars

bear skull

Bears have a stocky, muscular build and are very strong. Their body may look clumsy, but bears can run fast in short bursts.

Bears are **bowlegged**, which means their feet point toward each other. This position gives bears excellent grip and balance.

A bear's senses of hearing and sight are poor. Instead, the bear relies on its excellent sense of smell to locate food and danger.

Bear behavior

Although bears have different features and live in various habitats, their behavior is remarkably alike. Whether their home is a polar ice cap or a tropical rain forest, bears of different species act in similar ways.

Bears belong to the animal order **Carnivora**. Compared to other carnivores, however, most bears eat little meat. Instead, bears are **omnivores**, or animals that eat plants and meat. They feed on leaves, grasses, berries, insects, and even soft sapwood. In fact, only the polar bear is a true carnivore—it hunts seals.

Bears scratch their backs on trees to leave their scent. Their scent marks their home range and warns other bears to stay away.

Even the large grizzly has a diet that is made up mostly of grasses and berries.

Sweet tooth

Almost all bears love honey. They use their claws to rip open a beehive and eat the honey and **grubs**, or baby bees, inside. Even the angry, stinging bees do not disturb the bear. Some scientists think that the bear's fur is so thick that a bee's stinger cannot reach the bear's skin.

Familiar paths

The area in which a bear lives is called its **home range**. Depending on the species, a bear's range can be as small as ten square miles (26 square km), or larger than 1540 square miles (4000 square km)! A home range is often marked by well-worn trails. Some bears are creatures of habit and follow the same paths through their home range every year. They even place their feet in exactly the same spots each time they use a path.

Up a tree

Bears of smaller species climb well and love to play in trees. Their sharp, curved claws are perfect for gripping branches and trunks. Bears also escape up a tree when they sense danger. Sleepy sloth bears, sun bears, and spectacled bears even make themselves beds out of branches so they can sleep in trees.

When in danger, a mother bear will force her cubs to climb up a tree. The cubs wait in the tree until the danger has passed.

Winter sleep

Brown, polar, and black bears live in places with cold winters. Snow covers the ground, and it is difficult for the bears to find food. To survive this season, these bears spend most of the winter fast asleep.

To get ready for its long winter sleep, a bear eats as much food as possible. By the end of autumn, larger bears gain nearly 60 pounds (27 kg) of extra fat. This stored body fat provides the bear with food and water during its sleep.

One eye open

The winter sleep of bears is not quite the same as that of true **hibernators**, such as dormice. Hibernators do not wake up for several months. Still, a bear's body is well designed for its long sleep. The bear's heart rate slows down, and the animal does not have to eat, drink, or urinate at all throughout the winter.

During the winter, bears wake up on warmer days. The American black bear, above, is coming out of its den for a stretch.

The cosy den

Bears dig themselves a **den** for warmth and protection. They dig their den into the side of a riverbank or small hill. The den has a narrow entrance that leads to a cosy room for sleeping. The room is big enough for the bear to roll around and stretch. Some bears use a place that is already hollow, such as a cave.

The nursery

Mother bears usually give birth in January or February. Her cubs are born in the den. The den provides the tiny cubs with shelter from cold weather and protection from enemies. The mother's body heat helps keep the den warm. By late spring, the cubs are strong enough to go outside with their mother.

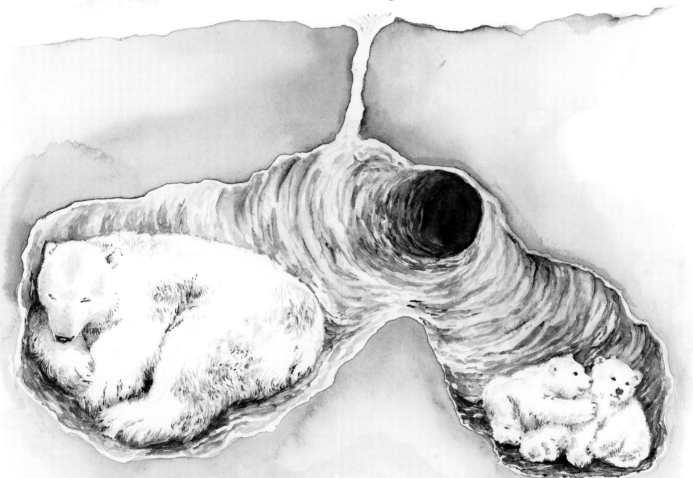

Inside this polar bear den, the tiny cubs play as their mother sleeps. She sleeps most of the time but wakes up to care for her cubs. The cubs nudge their mother when they want to feed.

Caring for cubs

When bear cubs are born, they are tiny, blind, and have little fur. They are usually born as twins or triplets in a group called a **litter**. Newborn cubs weigh under two pounds (0.9 kg), whereas their mother may weigh as much as 500 pounds (227 kg). The father does not see his cubs. These helpless animals rely on their mother for food and protection. Bear cubs are a favorite meal for wolves and even other adult bears.

Cubs call for their mother when they are frightened or hungry.

Cubs from the same litter are often different colors. This black bear sow has two brown cubs and one black cub.

It's all they need

For the first year or two of life, cubs drink nothing but their mother's milk. The mother bear sits down or lies on her back, and the cubs climb onto her chest to drink the milk. Bear milk is rich in fat, so the tiny cubs grow very quickly.

The best teacher

Cubs stay with their mother for at least a year and a half. Some cubs, such as grizzly cubs, stay with their mother for as long as three years. The cubs learn everything by watching their mother. If they are misbehaving, she smacks them firmly with her paw. She shows them which plants and berries are safe to eat, how to hunt and kill prey, and how to build a den.

Charge!

Female bears protect their cubs at all costs. Some even die defending their cubs from wolves or other bears, but that does not happen often. When confronted by an enemy, a sow roars loudly and charges. Animals know that an enraged mother bear is very dangerous. Her size and fierce roar are usually enough to scare away any intruders.

For protection, cubs stay by their mother's side for the first two years of their life.

Polar bears

The polar bear lives in one of the coldest places on Earth—the Arctic. This bear is well suited to its harsh environment. In fact, an adult polar bear can spend its entire life on huge ice **floes**, or sheets, that float on the Arctic Ocean.

*White fur blends in perfectly with the polar bear's snowy habitat. Coloring that helps hide an animal is called **camouflage**. Sometimes polar bears even cover their black nose with a paw as they sneak up on a seal.*

The polar bear's double-layered fur works in many ways to keep the bear warm. The hairs are hollow to trap heat, and their light color allows sunlight to travel through to the bear's body. Underneath, the bear's skin is black. Black is a color that **absorbs**, or collects, heat.

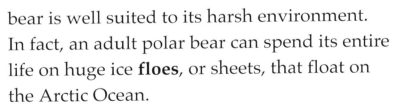

Patient hunters

Much of the Arctic Ocean is covered by ice. Seals cut breathing holes into the ice so they can surface for air. Polar bears hunt seals by waiting at these breathing holes. They crouch by a hole, wait, and sometimes do not move for hours. Once a seal's head pops up, the bear quickly grabs the seal with its claws, bites it, and drags it onto the ice.

The polar bear must stay alert as it waits. It has only a few seconds to grab the seal.

Perfect paws

A polar bear's feet are perfect for walking on cold, slippery ice. Unlike other bears, polar bears have a thick layer of fur on the bottom of their feet. Not only does this fur keep their feet warm, it also provides the bear with extra grip on the ice. Their toes are also slightly **webbed**, or connected by a flap of skin. This webbing allows the paws to act as a paddle when the bears swim.

Olympic swimmers

Although they are land-based animals, polar bears are incredible swimmers. They can swim up to 50 miles (80 km) away from shore before they need to return. Polar bears swim from place to place to find seals that they can hunt for food. When a polar bear gets out of the water, it quickly shakes itself dry so its coat will not freeze.

When the sea ice melts in the summer, polar bears swim hours at a time!

Brown bears

Brown bears live in more places than any other species of bear. These bears vary greatly in size— adults can be anywhere from five feet (1.5 m) to ten feet (3 m) in length. There are several kinds

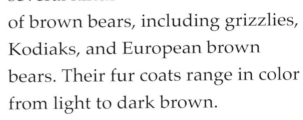

of brown bears, including grizzlies, Kodiaks, and European brown bears. Their fur coats range in color from light to dark brown.

The largest brown bears, such as Kodiaks and some grizzlies, are those that live near rivers and ocean coasts. These bears feed on large amounts of fish, as well as berries and grasses. Fish are high in **protein**, which helps these bears grow large. Some Kodiaks are as large as polar bears and weigh over 1000 pounds (450 kg).

The brown bears of the northwestern United States and Canada are the fishers of the bear world. In spring, they wade out into rivers and catch salmon that are swimming upstream to breed. Once they catch a fish, many bears eat only the skin and head. They leave the rest behind for other animals to eat.

Smaller cousins

European brown bears are smaller than their cousins in North America and Russia. They live in forests and feed on plants and small mammals such as rodents. There are few brown bears left in Europe because humans have driven them out of their habitat.

Sharp claws

A brown bear's long, straight claws are excellent for digging. Ground squirrels are among the bear's favorite foods. These squirrels live in underground homes called **burrows**. A brown bear can use its claws to dig a squirrel out of its burrow. The bear's claws are also dangerous weapons. Even large animals can be killed by a single blow from a brown bear's paw!

Brown bears have a large rounded hump above their shoulders. This hump is a muscle that the bear uses for digging. Grizzlies have a bigger hump than that of other brown bears.

A short rest

A brown bear spends much of its day resting. Its home range has several **day beds** that the bear uses for short naps. A day bed is a simple pile of twigs, leaves, and grasses. A napping bear never sleeps too soundly on its day bed. It must be on the alert for approaching enemies.

The fur of most grizzlies is blond-tipped and looks "grizzled," or frosted. Can you guess how these bears got their name?

American black bears

American black bears are found only in North America, yet there are more of them than any other bear in the world. These medium-sized bears come in a wide range of colors such as the reddish-brown color of the cinnamon black bear. The Kermodes black bear is actually light blond! Despite their different colors, all American black bears are the same size and have similar features. Black bears stay in the forest to avoid contact with the stronger grizzlies. Hungry grizzlies have been known to kill and eat black bears!

Leave no rock unturned

Black bears look everywhere when searching for food. Using their strong paws and sharp claws, they tear open tree stumps and flip over stones and logs. These places are full of tasty insects and larvae. Fruits, bird eggs, and honey are also favorite black bear meals. Bears that live near campsites often raid garbage cans and dumps searching for food.

Tree peelers

Some black bears peel the bark off trees to eat the soft sapwood underneath. Unfortunately, this practice damages the trees. For many years, forestry companies shot black bears to ensure that their trees would not be damaged. Today, some companies leave food for the bears so they will not harm the trees.

Teddy bears

Did you know that the original teddy bear was based on a real black bear? Once when U.S. President Theodore "Teddy" Roosevelt went hunting, he captured a black bear. He brought it home and kept it as a pet. The bear became popular, and a toy company made a stuffed imitation, which they called the "Teddy" bear.

On hot days, black bears love to swim and cool off in the water.

Black bears break open rotten logs and feast on the insects inside.

Asiatic black bears

The Asiatic black bear can be recognized by its large rounded ears and fluffy shoulder mane. This bear is similar in size to the American black bear and lives in mountain forests in many parts of Asia. It is also known as the "moon bear" because it has a crescent-shaped patch of pale fur on its chest.

Mountain bear

The Asiatic black bear is **nocturnal**— it is active mainly during the night. It spends its summer in the mountains. In warm weather, the bear eats mainly fruits and plants. It uses its climbing ability to pick tree fruit that many animals cannot reach.

In winter, the bear moves down to the bottom of the mountain where the temperature is warmer. Fruit is difficult to find in winter, so the bear hunts prey such as sheep, goats, and rodents. In places where the winter is very cold, the bear sleeps for several months.

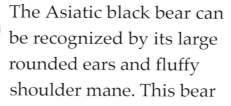

Sun bears

The world's smallest bear is the sun bear. This nocturnal bear lives in the tropical rain forests of Southeast Asia in countries such as Malaysia and Indonesia. The sun bear gets its name from the bright yellow patch of fur on its chest. Its love of honey has earned it another name—honey bear.

Hive raider

The sun bear's sharp, curved claws allow it to rip open beehives easily. The bear then uses its long, narrow tongue to lick out the sweet honey. Insects of all kinds are also on the sun bear's menu. It eats termites, ants, and larvae.

The sun bear has shorter fur than that of other bears because its habitat is warm all year. It does not sleep through the winter.

During the day, the sun bear breaks branches and builds itself a comfortable nest in a tree.

Spectacled bears

Have you ever seen a bear with **spectacles**, or eyeglasses? The pale rings of fur around the eyes of the spectacled bear look just like glasses! Spectacled bears are the only remaining short-faced bears. They have a shorter **muzzle**, or nose and mouth, than that of other bears. Their ancestors include the giant short-faced bear, which may have been the largest carnivorous mammal!

The spectacled bear is the only species that lives in South America. Its home is in the Andes Mountains, so this bear is also known as the Andean bear. It is a shy animal that is difficult to study. Like most small bear species, it spends much of its time in trees and eats more plants than meat.

(above) The eye and chest markings of spectacled bears differ from bear to bear.

Sloth bears

One of the more unusual bears is the sloth bear of India. When this bear was first discovered,  it was found hanging upside down in trees by its long, curved claws. This behavior and its long, shaggy fur led people to believe that this bear was actually a sloth. The sloth bear, however, is definitely a bear!

Vacuum mouth

Although this bear enjoys honey and berries, it eats mostly termites. Using its large claws, it smashes a hole in a termite mound. It then places its lips around the hole, curls its long tongue into a tube, and sucks the termites up into its mouth. The bear does not have two front teeth, making it easier for the animal to suck up food. The sound of a sloth bear sucking up insects is so loud, it can be heard 600 feet (183 m) away!

(right) Sloth bear cubs often have brown fur. Their fur becomes darker as they become adults.

The sloth bear uses its sense of smell to locate termites. It can close its nostrils to stop termites from going inside its nose.

Giant pandas

The rarest bear in the world is the giant panda. Panda mothers raise one cub at a time. If a second cub is born, it is left behind and dies. The giant panda is the least carnivorous of all bears—it rarely eats meat. It is a very picky eater! Its diet consists only of **bamboo**, a tall woody grass that grows in China.

Thumbs up!

Panda paws are different from those of other bears. There is an extra bone on the paw that acts as a thumb. Using its "thumb," the panda can grip **shoots**, or sticks, of bamboo as it eats.

Eat, eat, eat

Although parts of the panda's body are well adapted to eating bamboo, this plant is not a nutritious food. The panda's stomach has difficulty **digesting** the bamboo, or breaking it down into energy. Pandas need to eat as much as 80 pounds (36 kg) of bamboo a day to stay healthy.

The panda's jaw is very strong. This bear spends its whole day chewing bamboo.

Bears and people

People are both frightened and amazed by bears. Their size and strength make them powerful and sometimes dangerous. The more we learn about bears, however, the more we discover how intelligent these shy animals are!

Circus act

For many centuries, bear cubs were stolen from their mothers and raised by people. These people trained the bears to perform tricks. Brown bears were a common part of European circuses. On streets in India, owners made sloth bears perform for people. Trained bears were mistreated and beaten if they disobeyed. In most countries, it is now illegal to own bears.

Sloth bears were forced to dance for people on city streets.

Learning about bears

When studying bears, scientists try to use methods that do not harm the animal. Using special devices, scientists can track and study the bear in its natural habitat without disturbing it very much. Scientists are able to get close to the bears by using **tranquilizer** guns. Tranquilizers make a bear fall asleep so it will not attack. Once the bear is asleep, the scientists tag its ears and place a radio collar around its neck to keep track of the animal.

This polar bear's ears have been tagged by scientists. The tags are so small that they do not bother the bear.

Meeting bears

All species of bears prefer to avoid people. When camping or on a hike through bear country, however, there is always a chance you will meet a wild bear. A surprised bear can be dangerous, so it is best to leave it alone. Even if a bear appears friendly, do not ever feed or touch it. It may see your campsite as a good source of food and decide not to leave you alone.

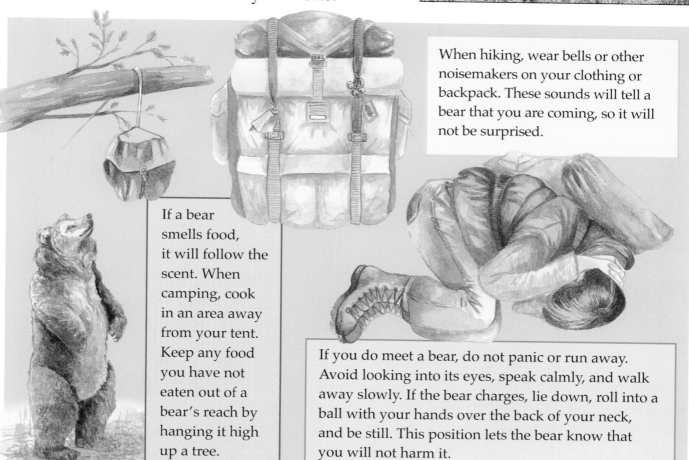

When hiking, wear bells or other noisemakers on your clothing or backpack. These sounds will tell a bear that you are coming, so it will not be surprised.

If a bear smells food, it will follow the scent. When camping, cook in an area away from your tent. Keep any food you have not eaten out of a bear's reach by hanging it high up a tree.

If you do meet a bear, do not panic or run away. Avoid looking into its eyes, speak calmly, and walk away slowly. If the bear charges, lie down, roll into a ball with your hands over the back of your neck, and be still. This position lets the bear know that you will not harm it.

Bears in danger

Sadly, bears all over the world are losing their habitat. Some bears such as the panda and spectacled bear are extremely rare. Although countries have laws to protect bears, many bears are hunted and trapped illegally.

Most bears live in a forest habitat, and many forests are threatened. When forests are cut down and replaced by towns or farms, the bears lose a part of their home. There is less wild forest space in which bears can live.

Every 50 years, bamboo forests flower, die, and slowly regrow. During this time, pandas in the forest are left without food. In the past, pandas moved to a new forest that was not flowering. Today, however, towns and farms have been built between forests. Often the pandas cannot travel through the towns to new forests, and they die of starvation.

(above) Illegally kept bears, such as this sun bear, often live in rundown cages. Many are abused by their owners.

Medicine bear

In China, some people believe that **bile** from the bear's **gall bladder** can be used for medicine. Asiatic black bears have been hunted for centuries for their gall bladders, paws, and bones. Now there are fewer of these bears left in the wild. Some people have started black bear farms. The bears are locked in cages and held permanently in one position for years. Tubes are inserted into their gall bladders so bile can be removed constantly from the animals.

Protecting the bears

Not all bears are in danger. Despite habitat loss, the polar bear population is on the rise. Anti-hunting laws are helping bears survive and have healthy cubs. National parks and reserves around the world are protecting the habitat of bears. Some, such as Denali National Park in Alaska, allow people to view grizzlies undisturbed in their natural habitat. To learn about the many bear-friendly organizations around the world, you can try an Internet search.

Melting away

Although the polar bear does not live in a forest, even its habitat is in danger. Each winter, giant sheets of **sea ice** form over Arctic waters. The bear depends on sea ice to hunt seals. In recent years, less and less sea ice has been forming. This change in the amount of ice makes it harder for polar bears to hunt the seals they need to stay healthy. In the future, some bears may find it difficult to locate the food they need to survive.

Words to know

bile A liquid found in an animal's gall bladder, which is used to help that animal digest food

boar An adult male bear

camouflage A color pattern on an animal that allows it to hide from enemies

canine One of an animal's long, curved front teeth which are used to tear flesh

carnivore An animal that eats mainly meat

den A shelter used especially during winter sleep

digest To break down food into nutrients to be used by the body as energy

guard hairs Long hairs that protect an animal's soft underfur and help keep the animal warm

hibernate To go into a heavy sleep during the winter months

litter A group of babies born to an animal at one time

molar One of an animal's flat back teeth, which are used to grind food

nocturnal Describing an animal that is active mainly at night

omnivore An animal that eats plants and animals

plantigrade Describing an animal that walks with its heels flat on the ground

protein A substance that is important for growth and is found in certain foods, especially meat

solitary Describing an animal that lives most of its life alone

sow An adult female bear

species A group of very similar living things that are capable of breeding

tranquilizer A gun-propelled dart used to make an animal become drowsy or fall asleep, so that scientists can study it safely

vertebrate An animal with a backbone

warm-blooded Describing an animal whose body temperature remains the same in hot or cold surroundings

Index

American black bears 6, 12, 14, 20-21, 22
ancestors 6, 24
Asiatic black bears 7, 12, 22, 31
behavior 10-11, 25
body 4, 8-9, 12, 13
brown bears 6, 18-19, 28, 31
camping 21, 29
claws 5, 7, 8, 11, 19, 21, 23, 25
cubs 11, 13, 14-15, 25, 26, 28, 31
dangers 9, 11, 30-31
dens 12, 13, 15
enemies 4, 7, 13, 15, 19
European brown bear 18, 19
food 5, 6, 7, 8, 9, 10, 11, 12, 14, 15, 18, 19, 21, 22, 23, 24, 25, 26, 29, 30, 31
forests 4, 6, 7, 10, 19, 20, 21, 22, 23, 30
fur 4, 8, 11, 16, 17, 18, 19, 22, 23, 24, 25
giant pandas 6, 7, 26-27, 30
grizzlies 4, 8, 10, 15, 18-19, 20
habitat 10, 16, 19, 23, 28, 30, 31
home range 10, 11, 19
hunting 10, 15, 17, 22, 25, 31
Kermodes black bear 20
Kodiaks 4, 6, 18
mating 5
milk 4, 13, 15
mountains 7, 22, 24
people 5, 19, 25, 28-29, 31
polar bears 4, 6, 10, 13, 16-17, 18, 28, 31
protection 12, 14, 15, 30, 31
seasons 12-13, 17, 18, 22, 23, 31
senses 9, 11, 25
sleeping 11, 12,-13, 19, 22, 23
sloth bears 7, 11, 25, 28
spectacled bears 5, 7, 11, 24, 30
sun bears 7, 11, 23, 30
swimming 17, 21

1 2 3 4 5 6 7 8 9 0   Printed in the U.S.A.   0 9 8 7 6 5 4 3 2 1